MAKING CANDLES

This edition published 2022

Search Press Limited
Wellwood, North Farm Road,
Tunbridge Wells, Kent TN2 3DR

First published as *Making Candles: Create 20 decorative candles to keep or give* in 2017; reprinted in 2019

Text copyright © Sarah Ditchfield 2022
Photographs by Paul Bricknell and Fiona Murray
for Search Press

Photographs and design copyright © Search Press Ltd 2022

ISBN: 978-1-80092-023-1
ebook ISBN: 978-1-80093-013-1

The Publishers and author can accept no responsibility for any consequences arising from the information, advice or instructions given in this publication.

Readers are permitted to reproduce any of the items in this book for their personal use, or for the purposes of selling for charity, free of charge and without the prior permission of the Publishers. Any use of the items for commercial purposes is not permitted without the prior permission of the Publishers.

You are invited to the author's website:
www.candlebyevents.co.uk

Suppliers

For details of suppliers, please visit the Search Press website: www.searchpress.com

If you would like further help or guidance with sourcing supplies please contact Sarah, who is happy to suggest suppliers: contact@candlebyevents.co.uk

Publisher's note

All the step-by-step photographs in this book feature the author, Sarah Ditchfield, demonstrating how to make candles. No models have been used.

DEDICATION

This book is dedicated to my husband, Philip, who bought me the candle-making kit for Christmas that unleashed my passion for candle-making, and to my two beautiful children Louise and Christopher.

ACKNOWLEDGMENTS

I would like to thank all of the Search Press staff for their fabulous collaboration on this book.

MAKING CANDLES

20 easy projects for a relaxing home

Sarah Ditchfield

Search Press

CONTENTS

INTRODUCTION

The first candles date back before 3000BC and were made by Ancient Egyptians. These candles were made out of reeds, which were dipped into melted animal fat called tallow. In years gone by, chandlers (candle-makers) were very sought-after, as they created light in homes. Even after the discovery of electricity, the candle industry continued to grow. Today, candles are used symbolically in many religions, and for celebrations, commemorations and, of course, relaxation.

In this book I will show you, step by step, how to create many different types of candle. You may become an amateur or perhaps even a professional chandler, bringing light into your home – and into those of other people too. My hope is that this book will be your go-to guide for candle-making and will inspire you to create your own projects – and if you do so, I would be delighted to hear from you!

At the beginning I will introduce all the tools and materials you will need. This will be followed by a chapter of basic techniques to get you started. Then we move on to projects that you can work through to practise and perfect your candle-making skills. Finally, we touch upon some ideas for decorating and packaging your candles to give them a professional look.

Candle-making does not have to be an expensive pastime – in fact, I have included a short section on upcycling materials – things you can find in your home that can be used for making candles.

The best thing about candle-making is that it's fun and creative, and relaxing for adults and children alike. I've taught candle-making to a variety of people over the years; men in particular often enjoy the 'science' around candle-making. My husband and I have often made candles in the evening over a glass of wine, and some of the designs in this book – including the ice pillar candle on page 62 – were perfected during those early evening experiments!

I hope you also find candle-making a wonderful pastime. Perhaps you will even take it to the next level and become a professional chandler.

Happy candle-making!

COMPLEXITY

To help you decide which projects to tackle as you hone your skills, I have graded the techniques by complexity:

simple

moderate

more challenging

NOTE

If this book inspires you to design and create your own candles to sell, you will need to ensure that they comply with the classification, labelling and packaging legislation in your country of residence.

Beeswax sheets

TOOLS AND MATERIALS

You will need quite a few tools for making candles. However, you will find that you already have most of these items in your home. Any additional items are fairly inexpensive to buy. The most important outlay when making candles is the key ingredient: wax.

WAXES

There are many different types of wax available. The most widely used wax is petroleum, but there are also a number of natural waxes such as soy wax, beeswax and rapeseed. If you are burning a lot of candles, natural wax is better for you and for your home. Each of these waxes comes with its own advantages and challenges, depending on how you want to use it.

Beeswax pellets

Petroleum wax (pillar)

Petroleum wax (container)

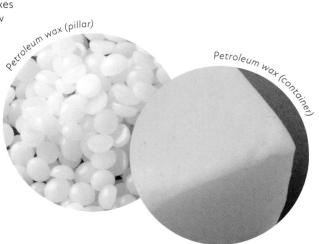

Beeswax

Beeswax is a natural product formed from the secretion of worker honey bees. When the beekeeper removes the honey from the hive, the leftover hexagonal wax cells are melted down and used for making candle wax. Beeswax is yellow-gold in colour and its sweet smell varies depending on the flowers and plants from which the bees have fed.

You can make container, pillar and simple rolled candles (see pages 32–33) using beeswax sheets: the latter are great for making with young children as they do not involve melting wax.

Petroleum wax

Petroleum wax (also called paraffin wax) is a by-product of the oil industry and is white in colour.

Petroleum wax is probably the most widely used wax, although it comes with its challenges. It can be sooty – particularly if too large a wick is used. Petroleum wax is also more difficult to clean out of your pans and equipment.

However, petroleum wax is a great wax to work with, particularly when making taper candles. You can also twist and mould your designs, as petroleum wax is malleable. The wax comes in the form of pellets and blocks (see above).

Rapeseed wax pellets

Soy wax flakes

Rapeseed wax

Rapeseed wax is a natural vegetable wax made from the yellow flower of the rapeseed plant. It comes in pellet form (as shown above) or in blocks.

A NOTE ABOUT WAXES

You can interchange many of the waxes used in the projects that follow; for instance, you can use petroleum wax instead of soy wax (or vice versa). However, you must ensure that you use the correct wick for the wax – and always burn test your candles (see page 78).

Soy wax

I tend to use soy wax in most of my workshops. It is made from soya beans and produces a cream-coloured candle. The benefit of soy wax is that it is biodegradable; it also produces no toxins and much less soot than petroleum candles. However, it is less malleable than petroleum wax (opposite) so if you are making taper candles you may need to practise with this wax for a while before you succeed.

As soy wax is water-soluble it can be washed away easily from your equipment with soap and hot water; spills are also fairly easy to wash away. Soy wax is also kosher-certified.

Soy wax can be purchased as flakes (as seen above) or in pellet form. It is available as both container and pillar wax.

Gel wax

Gel wax

Candle gel is made from mineral oils and a polymer resin that turns the oil to a gelatinous composition, and gives it a clear, rubbery texture. Gel candles tend to burn for twice as long as petroleum candles. As gel is transparent you can achieve some beautiful effects with your candles.

CONTAINER WAX OR PILLAR WAX?

Container candles are lit and burned inside a container, such as a votive holder, a glass tumbler or even a coconut shell (see page 22). When making a container candle, you should use a container wax: this wax adheres to the sides of the container and does not shrink when the candle is cooling.

Pillar candles are self-contained, free-standing candles. Pillar wax is slightly harder than container wax and shrinks when cooling – this allows you to remove the candle more easily from its mould once it has set.

Never use container wax in a candle mould as it is likely to stick to the mould, and you will struggle to remove the finished candle.

CANDLE MOULDS AND CONTAINERS

Moulds

Candle moulds come in many different shapes and sizes. They are used for creating pillar candles. Moulds are typically made from metal, polycarbonate, plastic, latex or silicone, and can be bought through specialist suppliers.

Containers

A candle container 'contains' the finished candle. The types of container are almost limitless: they just need to be able to withstand the heat of the melted wax and flame. Typical containers include glass tumblers, votive holders and tins but you can use more unusual receptacles such as shells and bottle tops. See page 72 for more inspiration. Some forms of plastic, like heat-resistant acrylic, work well for candles – but be careful when using plastic containers, and check that they are heat-resistant first. You must always burn test your candles (see page 78) before giving them as presents or selling them.

You can buy clear polycarbonate tealight containers in a variety of shapes, including round and heart-shaped, which are used for the Valentine tealight project on page 34.

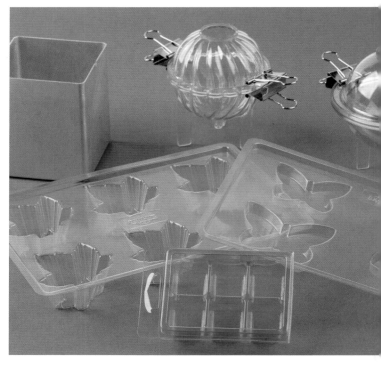

Candle moulds

Clockwise, from top left: square metal mould, fluted and plain sphere moulds, butterfly mould tray, clamshell mould and maple leaf mould tray.

Candle containers

Clockwise from top left: flowerpot, Mason glass, glass tumblers, heart tealight container and coconut shell.

WICKS AND SUSTAINERS

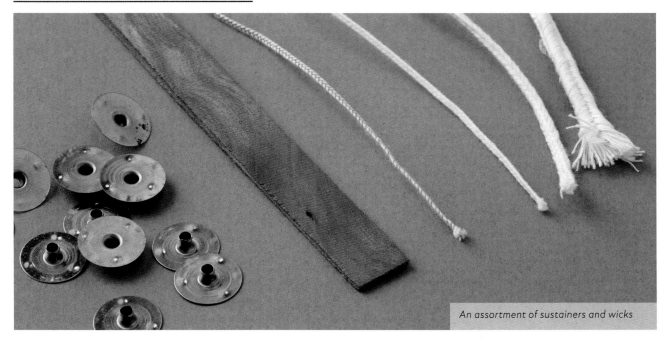

An assortment of sustainers and wicks

Wicks

Wicks are designed to draw melted wax upwards and to burn safely. Although most wicks look like lengths of string, they are made specifically for candles, and generally made from cotton or wood. They come in many different shapes, weaves and materials, ranging from flat-braided or square cotton wicks to wooden or cored wicks.

The size of wick you need depends on the diameter of the candle, the size of the melt pool you require (see note, below) and the type of wax and fragrance oil used. A wick supplier can recommend the most appropriate wick for your purposes; however, for each of the projects in this book I have specified the most suitable wick.

If you choose a wick that is too thick (or big) the candle will burn too quickly and will mushroom, and will emit too much soot and smoke. If your wick is too thin (or small) the flame will not establish fully. Solutions to these issues and more can be found on page 79, under 'Troubleshooting'.

You can experiment with different types and sizes of wick to see which ones give the best results.

Sustainers

These are small pieces of metal, with a hole in the middle. The sustainer is secured to the wick (see page 17) and attached to the bottom of a candle container.

'MUSHROOMING'

The wick develops build-ups that look like mushrooms.

MELT POOL

This is the pool of melted wax you see on the top of a candle, around the wick. For a correctly wicked candle, this pool should extend to the inner diameter of the container or close to the edge of the pillar; this creates a nice effect as the candle burns. Generally, melt pools are around 1–2cm (⅜-¾in) in depth, depending on the candle type.

Wicking pins and sticks

Wicking pins and sticks, which hold a wick in place at the top of a container candle or mould, can be bought from specialist candle-making suppliers. Alternatively, you can make your own wicking sticks using two wooden coffee stirrers and two small elastic bands (see page 17).

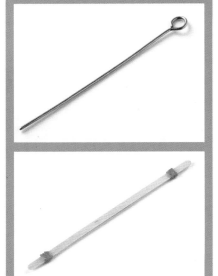

Preparation tools

Measuring jugs

Double boiler

Metal dipping pot in tall saucepan

Wicking tools

PREPARATION TOOLS

Baking tray

This protects your work surface and is great for catching any spillages.

Chopping board

This is an ideal surface on which to roll and trim beeswax sheets (see pages 32–33).

Funnels

A funnel is particularly useful for pouring wax beads into a candle container (see pages 36–37).

Metal jug

Use a metal jug to pour melted, hot wax into your mould or container. Make sure the jug can withstand the temperature of the hot wax, and is a good pourer.

Scales

These are used for weighing wax, dye chips and fragrance oil.

Spoon and palette knife

Use a wooden or metal spoon and a metal palette knife to stir wax.

Thermometer

Ideally, use a thermometer that can measure up to 100°C (212°F), such as a cook's thermometer.

MEASURING JUGS

These are used for calculating the amount of wax required.

WICKING TOOLS

Crimping tool

This tool secures the wick to the sustainer (see page 17).

Scissors

These are used for cutting wicks. I prefer to use small, very sharp scissors.

Metal ruler

Use a ruler to measure wicks and beeswax sheets that are to be cut.

DOUBLE BOILER

You can buy one of these from a specialist supplier or cook shop, or simply use a large pan with a small pan or heat-resistant bowl on top. See page 15 for more instructions on using the double boiler.

POTS AND PANS

Metal dipping pot (optional)

You will need a tall, narrow container if you are making dipped taper candles (see pages 60–61); asparagus boilers work well.

Tall saucepan

When using a tall saucepan, place a metal trivet inside to support the metal dipping pot.

ADDITIONAL TOOLS

Apron

To protect your clothing.

Oven gloves

For handling hot pans, containers and metal jugs of wax.

Adhesive putty

For sealing holes in candle moulds.

Glue dots

For attaching the sustainer to the candle container.

TECHNIQUES

You will need to apply these techniques to most, if not all, of the projects in this book. Keep this book close by as you make your first candles, as a quick and easy point of reference.

MELTING WAX

How to calculate the right amount of wax

The easiest way to establish how much wax you need is to fill your mould or container with water.

1 If you are using a mould, make sure you block off the hole in the bottom with adhesive putty, otherwise water will escape.

2 Fill the mould to the top with water. Then pour the water into a measuring jug and make a note of the volume.

Convert the volume of your mould in millilitres into grams, at a ratio of 1:1; for example

100ml (3½fl.oz) equals 100g (3½oz)

Melted wax weighs about 10 per cent less than water so you need to reduce the amount of wax by 10 per cent.

If you have the equivalent of 100g (3½oz) of water you will need

100g – 10% (10g) = 90g

In imperial measurements, this equates roughly to:

3½oz – 10% (¼oz) = 3¼oz

You can also use the following table:

Volume of water	Volume of wax flakes
100g (3½oz)	90g (3¼oz)
200g (7oz)	180g (6½oz)
300g (10½oz)	270g (9½oz)
400g (14oz)	360g (12¾oz)
500g (17½oz)	450g (15¾oz)
600g (21oz)	540g (19oz)
700g (24½oz)	630g (22¼oz)
800g (28oz)	720g (25½oz)
900g (31¾oz)	810g (28½oz)
1000g (35¼oz)	900g (31¾oz)

Melting wax with a double boiler

The safest way to melt wax is to use a double boiler. This can be bought from a specialist supplier or cook shop – or you can use a large pan with a small pan (or heat-resistant bowl) on top. Bring the water to simmering point, add the wax to the top pan (or bowl) and stir occasionally with a spoon as the wax starts to melt.

As a rough guide the melting points and pouring temperatures are:

Wax	Melting point temperature	Max. heating temperature	Pouring temperature
Beeswax	62°C (144 °F)	80°C (176°F)	75°C (167°F)
Soy	50°C (122°F)	70°C (158°F)	60°C (140°F)
Petroleum	57°C (135°F)	80°C (176°F)	75°C (167°F)
Gel wax	70°C (158°F)	80°C (176°F)	75°C (167°F)

Always refer to the manufacturer's guidelines when heating wax. If you are heating large quantities of wax, you can also buy purpose-made wax melters. Although these can be expensive, they are thermostatically controlled so you can pre-set the temperature.

IMPORTANT SAFETY INSTRUCTIONS

Melting wax safely

- Never melt wax on direct heat – always use a double boiler.
- Never leave wax unattended when heating.
- Do not let the temperature of wax exceed 93°C (199°F). To test the temperature of the wax, use a craft or cook's thermometer (see Preparation tools, page 13).
- Never pour water onto a wax or oil fire as this can cause an explosion.

Burning candles safely

- Remove all packaging before lighting.
- Place candles on a heat-resistant surface.
- Keep wick upright and trimmed to 5mm (¼in).
- Do not place anything on top of the candle.
- Extinguish candle when only 5mm (¼in) of wax remains.
- Burn candles in a ventilated room.
- Never leave a candle burning unattended.
- Keep candles away from draughts and flammable materials.
- Keep candles out of reach of children and pets.
- Store candles away from sunlight and heat.
- Do not burn candles longer than three hours at a time.

NOTES

Candle wax has a flashpoint – the point at which it will catch fire – so always refer to the wax manufacturer's guidelines. The actual flashpoint depends on the type of wax and any additives in the wax. Keeping the temperature below 93°C (199°F) and using a double boiler (ensuring the bottom pan contains water) will mean that your wax will not get too hot.

Well before wax catches fire it does tend to smell, turn brown and generate smoke. If you ever experience a wax or oil fire, turn off the heat immediately and cover the pan with a lid, fire blanket or damp (not wet) tea towel. Protect your hands when placing any item on the fire.

PREPARING A CANDLE MOULD OR CONTAINER

If you are making your own mould you will need to make a small hole in the bottom of the mould for the wick to feed through. Place a cork mat on your work surface, and use a skewer or bradawl to make a hole in the mould.

Ensure your containers or moulds are at room temperature before you pour your wax; and pour slowly to avoid creating air bubbles.

PREPARING THE WICK

Priming the wick

Priming is pre-coating the wick with wax. If you do not prime a wick there is a good chance the wick will not work and will simply burn before it has a chance to melt and draw the liquid wax up to the flame. To avoid this, container candles require a primed wick. You can either buy wicks already primed or prime your own. If you want to do it yourself, here is how:

1 Melt a small amount of wax in a double boiler.

2 Submerge the entire wick in the melted wax. You will see small bubbles release from the wick as it absorbs the wax.

3 When there are no more bubbles, use a wicking stick to remove the wick from the pan. Hold the wick over the pan so that any excess wax drops back into the pan. Allow the wick to cool for a few seconds. As it cools, pull the wick at both ends to straighten.

Securing the wick to the base of a container

To ensure that the wick sits in the centre of the candle, you need to attach it to a sustainer.

1 Feed the primed wick through the hole in the middle of the sustainer.

2 Secure the wick to the sustainer using a crimping tool. Avoid leaving any wick protruding from the bottom of the sustainer as this makes it harder to secure the sustainer to your container. Trim off any excess with small, sharp scissors.

3 Stick a glue dot to the base of the sustainer (see inset), then stick the sustainer into the centre of the bottom of the container. You may need to use a wicking stick to push the sustainer down into place.

Securing the wick to a mould

1 Cut the wick about 10cm (4in) longer than the depth of the mould and thread it through the hole in the base.

2 Tie a knot in the wick on the underside of the mould to stop the wick from being pulled through. Seal the underside of the hole with adhesive putty.

Making wicking sticks

To ensure the wick stays upright you need a wicking pin or sticks. Wicking sticks are very easy to make, using two wooden coffee stirrers and two small elastic bands.

Join together the ends of the two coffee stirrers with the small elastic bands.

Thread the wick between the sticks to hold it in the centre of the mould or container when pouring the wax.

ADDING DYE

Dyes are available in chip, flake and liquid forms. Chips and flakes are easy to cut and measure. Liquid is very concentrated, and although you need only a few drops to colour your candles, it is more difficult to measure, so it can be challenging to create several batches in the same colour with liquid dye. Throughout this book we have used individual dye chips, which weigh 1g, but you can use and measure out liquid or flakes of dye as appropriate. As a rule of thumb, one chip of dye will colour about 100g (3½oz) of wax.

You can also use wax crayons to colour your candles (see pages 52–55 for an example).

Candle dyes in liquid, flake and chip form.

1 Melt the wax to the required temperature.

2 Pour the wax carefully into the metal jug.

3 Add the dye to the melted wax.

4 Stir the dye into the wax gently to avoid introducing air into your candles.

ADDING FRAGRANCE OIL

There are two types of fragrance oil: synthetic blends or essential oils (extracted from plants and flowers). Essential oils are more expensive than synthetic fragrance oils, but the fragrance is 100 per cent pure. You must ensure that the oils you use are suitable for candle-making. Read the manufacturer's guidelines and always burn test your candles before giving or selling them to others (see page 78 for more on burn testing).

The amount of fragrance you need is usually specified by the supplier. However, as a guide, you will need between 5–10 per cent of the weight of the wax.

Experiment and test your candles (see page 78) to make sure you get the correct 'throw', which is another way of saying, ensure that the smell is strong enough but not too strong.

Fragrance oils

Add the fragrance oil to the hot wax just before pouring the wax into the container or mould. By adding fragrance after the dye you avoid losing too much scent to the atmosphere before your candles have set.

BEEHIVE CANDLE

Beeswax is a lovely, natural material to work with – and smells of honey – so there is no need to add any fragrance. Simply enjoy the sweet smell of a wonderful wax.

You will need:

- **MOULD** Silicone beehive mould (4.5cm/1¾in diameter, 5.5cm/2¼in height)
- **WAX** 50g (1¾oz) beeswax
- **WICK** WickWell NT14
- Adhesive putty
- Double boiler
- Measuring jug
- Metal jug
- Spoon
- Scales
- Scissors
- Thermometer
- Wicking sticks

INSTRUCTIONS

1 Melt the beeswax in the double boiler.

2 Prime the wick.

3 Prepare the mould. Tie off the wick and seal the hole with adhesive putty. Secure the top of the wick using wicking sticks.

4 Once the wax has melted and is at 80°C (176°F), decant the melted wax into the metal jug. Do not overheat the wax: if the temperature goes above 85°C (185°F) it can discolour.

5 Check the wax temperature. It should now be around 75°C (167°F). If not, wait for it to cool to this temperature.

6 Slowly pour the wax into the beehive mould.

7 Tap the mould to release any air bubbles and check the wick is centred.

8 Now leave the candles to set fully. Depending on the ambient temperature, this will take about two hours.

9 When the candle has set, remove the wicking sticks, turn the mould upside-down and remove any adhesive putty. Untie the knot.

Silicone beehive mould

TIP

After step 6, save a small amount of wax in the jug – sometimes, once the candle has set, the base of the candle (uppermost in the mould) may have shrunk and become slightly concave. If this happens, heat the wax you saved earlier and pour it into the small concave dip. See page 30 for further instructions.

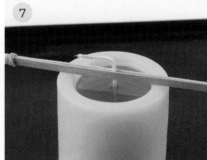

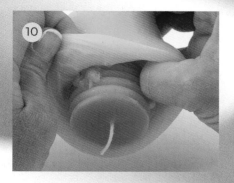

10 Pull back the silicone mould to release the candle. It will have shrunk slightly so should slide easily out of the mould.

11 Finally, trim the wick to 5mm (¼in).

COCONUT SHELL

The types of container you can use for your candles are limited only by your imagination. These containers make your candles truly tropical!

You will need:

- **CONTAINER**
  Coconut shell, washed

- **WAX**
  60g (2oz) soy container wax

- **WICK** Wedo Eco 14, primed, and sustainer

- **FRAGRANCE** 5g (¼oz) coconut candle fragrance oil

- Double boiler
- Glue dot
- Measuring jug
- Metal jug
- Scales
- Scissors
- Spoon
- Thermometer
- Wicking sticks

INSTRUCTIONS

1 Melt the soy container wax in the double boiler.

2 Prepare the wick and sustainer. Secure the wick to the base of the coconut shell using a glue dot. Secure the top of the wick with wicking sticks.

3 Once the wax has melted and is at 70°C (158°F), decant the melted wax into the metal jug.

4 Let the wax cool slightly to around 60°C (140°F), then add the coconut fragrance oil to the jug and stir.

5 Slowly pour the wax into the coconut shell.

6 Leave the candle to set fully. Depending on the ambient temperature, this will take about two hours.

7 Once set, remove the wicking sticks and trim the wick to 5mm (¼in).

FLOWERPOT WITH WOOD WICK

As the name suggests, wood wicks are made from wood; they will make your candles look expensive – and when lit they make a crackling sound similar to a campfire.

You will need:

- **CONTAINER** Flowerpot, 10cm (4in) diameter
- **WAX** 350g (12¼oz) soy container wax
- **WICK** Medium wood wick and wood wick sustainer
- **FRAGRANCE** 28g (1oz) citronella candle fragrance oil
- Adhesive putty
- Double boiler
- Measuring jug
- Metal jug
- Scales
- Scissors
- Spoon
- Thermometer

INSTRUCTIONS

1 Melt the soy container wax in the double boiler.

2 If your pot has a hole in the bottom, seal the hole with adhesive putty.

3 Slot the wood wick into the wood wick sustainer.

4 Stick the sustainer to the adhesive putty in the middle of the flowerpot.

5 Once the wax has melted and is at 70°C (158°F), decant the melted wax into the metal jug.

6 Check the wax temperature – it should now be around 60°C (140°F). If not, wait for it to cool to this temperature. Add the citronella fragrance oil to the jug and stir.

7 Slowly pour the wax into the flowerpot.

8 Leave the candle to set fully. Depending on the ambient temperature, this will take about two hours.

9 Once the candle has set, trim the wood wick to 5mm (¼in) using sharp scissors.

Wood wick and sustainer

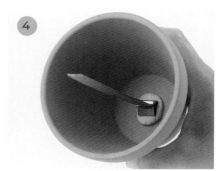

MASON GLASS CANDLE

You will need:

- **CONTAINER** Mason glass
- **WAX** 405g (14¼oz) PRO rapeseed container wax
- **WICK** Wedo ECO 12, primed, and sustainer
- **DYE** Yellow candle dye (see page 18 for directions on calculating amount of dye)
- **FRAGRANCE** 33g (1¼oz) tropical candle fragrance oil
- Double boiler
- Glue dot
- Measuring jug
- Metal jug
- Scales
- Scissors
- Spoon
- Thermometer
- Wicking sticks

Mason glasses, invented in 1858, with their screw lids, make fun candle containers. If you use a natural wax, like rapeseed, you can wash the glass with soap and water after you have burnt the candle, so you can use the container again and again.

For this project we are using PRO rapeseed container wax, which also contains small amounts of palm wax, beeswax and castor oil.

INSTRUCTIONS

1 Melt the PRO rapeseed container wax in the double boiler.

2 Prepare the wick and sustainer. Attach the sustainer to the inside base of the Mason glass with a glue dot.

3 Secure the wick with wicking sticks.

4 Once the wax has melted and is about 70°C (158°F), decant the melted wax into the metal jug. Add the yellow candle dye to the jug and stir gently until the dye has dissolved.

5 Let the wax cool to around 55°C (131°F), then add the tropical fragrance oil to the jug and stir.

6 Slowly pour the wax into the Mason glass. Save a small amount of wax in the jug – this particular wax can shrink so you may need to top up the candle once set.

7 Leave the candle to set fully. Depending on the ambient temperature, this will take about two hours.

8 Finally, trim the wick to 5mm (¼in).

OCTAGON PILLAR CANDLE

You will need:

- **MOULD** Metal octagon mould: 9cm (3½in) height, 8cm (3¼in) diameter
- **WAX** 400g (14oz) soy pillar wax
- **WICK** Wedo ECO 4
- **DYE** Purple candle dye (see page 18 for directions on calculating amount of dye)
- Adhesive putty
- Double boiler
- Measuring jug
- Metal jug
- Scales
- Scissors
- Spoon
- Thermometer
- Wicking sticks

Pillar candles are one of the most popular types of candle. Here, we are using an octagon mould to create a more unusual shape – however, the process is pretty much the same whatever mould you choose.

INSTRUCTIONS

1 Melt the soy pillar wax in the double boiler.

2 Prepare the mould. Tie off the wick and seal the hole with adhesive putty. Secure the top of the wick using wicking sticks.

3 Once the wax has melted and is at about 70°C (158°F), decant the melted wax into the metal jug. Add the purple candle dye to the jug and stir gently until the dye has dissolved.

4 Let the wax cool slightly to around 60°C (140°F), then slowly pour the wax into the octagon mould. Save a small amount of wax in the jug – you might need this later (see step 7).

5 Tap the mould to release any air bubbles and check the wick is centred.

6 Now leave the candle to set fully. Depending on the ambient temperature, this will take about two hours.

Metal octagon mould

The finished candle

The lilac hue of this particular candle makes it perfect for a relaxing, mindful environment. Why not add lavender oil to the wax to make this candle the ideal accompaniment for rest and relaxation?

7 Sometimes, once the candle has set, the base of the candle (uppermost in the mould) may have shrunk and become slightly concave or have holes (air pockets). If this happens, reheat the wax you saved earlier.

a Remove the wicking sticks.

b Pour the wax into the small concave dip. Leave the wax to set.

TIP

Do not fill beyond the edge of the dip with the excess wax, as the candle will have shrunk in the mould: any additional wax will run down the side between the mould and the candle, creating an unpleasant wax line.

8 When the candle has set, turn the mould upside-down. Remove the adhesive putty and untie the knot.

9 The candle will have shrunk slightly so it should easily slide out of the mould.

10 Finally, trim the wick to 5mm (¼in).

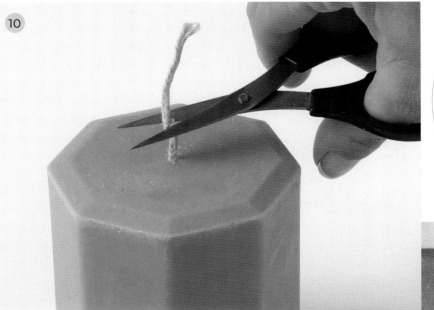

TIP

If you struggle to remove the candle from the mould, put the candle and mould in the freezer for 15 minutes. The candle should now come out easily. If not, return the candle, in the mould, to the freezer for another 15 minutes.

ROLLED BEESWAX CANDLE

This is an excellent candle to make with young children as there is no melting of wax involved. However, beeswax candles do drip when they burn so make sure you place the candle on a heat-resistant surface when it is lit.

Follow these instructions to make a straight candle from two single sheets of beeswax.

You will need:

- **WAX** 2 different coloured beeswax sheets
- **WICK** Wedo VRL 5, primed
- Chopping board
- Metal ruler
- Scissors, craft knife or sugarcraft cutters

TIP

Keep beeswax sheets at room temperature. If they are cold they are more difficult to roll and can crack.

INSTRUCTIONS

1 Put one beeswax sheet on the chopping board. Using a metal ruler as a guide, cut the sheet with a craft knife. The sheet should measure approximately 20 x 14cm (7¾ x 5½in).

2 Lay the wick along the longer side, 5mm (¼in) from the edge of the wax sheet.

3 Gently fold over the edge to cover the wick. Continue rolling until you reach the end of the sheet.

4 Roll the candle between your palms or your fingers to press down the seam, so that the candle does not unwind. Make sure that the bottom of the candle remains flat.

5 Trim the wick to 5mm (¼in).

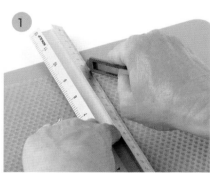

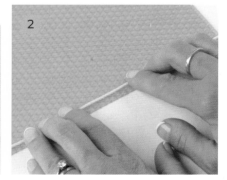

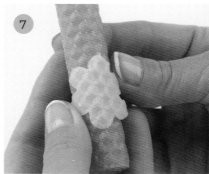

6 Decorate the candle by cutting shapes out of a second beeswax sheet using scissors, a craft knife or sugarcraft cutters (used for decorating cakes). Cut out some larger, paler flowers from a separate sheet, and smaller, darker flowers from the original beeswax sheet.

7 Finally, press the shapes firmly onto the beeswax candle.

The finished candle

Make the tapered candle on the right by layering two different coloured beeswax sheets, cutting them into identical triangles, placing a wick along one of the shorter sides, then rolling the two sheets together in the same way as shown in steps 3 and 4.

VALENTINE HEART TEALIGHTS

You will need:

- **CONTAINERS** 4 heart-shaped tealight containers
- **WAX** 135g (4¾oz) soy container wax
- **WICKS** 4 x Wedo TL25 wicks, primed, plus sustainers
- **DYE** Red candle dye (use one dye chip to make all four tealights)
- Candle glitter
- Double boiler
- Measuring jug
- Metal jug
- Scales
- Scissors
- Spoon
- Thermometer
- Optional: coffee stirrer

As well as regular round tealight containers, you can buy clear polycarbonate tealight containers in other shapes. For this project we are making heart-shaped tealights.

INSTRUCTIONS

1 Melt the soy container wax in the double boiler.

2 Prepare a wick and sustainer for each tealight.

3 Once the wax has melted and is around 70°C (158°F), decant the melted wax into the metal jug.

4 Add the red candle dye to the jug and stir gently until the dye has dissolved.

5 Let the wax cool slightly to around 60°C (140°F), then slowly pour the wax into the heart tealight containers.

6 While the wax is still translucent, carefully lower a wick and sustainer into the centre of each tealight container. Leave to set.

7 When the candles start to feel tacky (after about 15 minutes), sprinkle candle glitter over the surface to create the sparkle. You may find it easier to sprinkle the glitter using a coffee stirrer.

8 Leave the candles to set fully. Depending on the ambient temperature, this will take about 30 minutes. Once set, trim the wicks to 5mm (¼in).

Happy Valentine's Day!

Candle glitter

You can buy candle glitter from specialist suppliers. Glitter looks great on a candle and gives it a little extra sparkle.

WAX BEAD CANDLE

This is a fun, easy candle and is perfect to make with young children as you do not need to melt the wax to create the candle. Layer the coloured wax beads to create a pretty effect.

You will need:

- **CONTAINER** Glass tumbler (9cm/3½in height, 8cm/3¼in diameter)
- **WAX** 5 x 50g (1¾oz) wax beads in the following colours: white, pink, blue, green and yellow
- **WICK** Wedo ECO 16, primed, and sustainer
- Funnel
- Glue dot
- Scales
- Scissors
- Teaspoon
- Wicking sticks
- Optional: heat tool

INSTRUCTIONS

1 Prepare the wick and sustainer. Secure the top of the wick using wicking sticks.

2 Place the funnel over the glass tumbler and, using a teaspoon, spoon some of the white beads through the funnel, into the tumbler.

3 Now choose your next colour of wax beads – e.g. pink. As before, place the funnel over the glass tumbler and spoon the pink beads into the funnel.

4 Repeat this process using the other three colours until you are left with a 1cm (½in) gap at the top of the tumbler. Rotate the tumbler after adding each layer to ensure that the bead layers are relatively even.

5 Remove the wicking sticks. Trim the wick to 5mm (¼in). Once you have lit the candle for the first time, the top surface should melt and create a seal so the beads will not fall out. Alternatively, seal the top of the candle by applying heat with a heat tool, as shown.

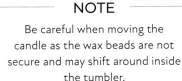

NOTE
Be careful when moving the candle as the wax beads are not secure and may shift around inside the tumbler.

CLAMSHELL ROSE PETAL WAX MELTS

You will need:

- **MOULD** Clamshell mould
- **WAX** 50g (1¾oz) soy pillar wax
- **DYE** Pale pink candle dye (see page 18 for directions on calculating amount of dye)
- **FRAGRANCE** 4g (¼oz) rose petal candle fragrance oil
- Double boiler
- Measuring jug
- Metal jug
- Scales
- Spoon
- Thermometer

Wax melts are used in oil burners. Rather than adding oil to the top of a burner you use a wax melt instead. Light the tealight candle underneath and wait for the wax above to melt.

Clamshell moulds tend to have six compartments. Pour the wax into each of the mould's compartments and wait for them to set. You can then easily break off a square and place it on the oil burner.

INSTRUCTIONS

1 Melt the soy pillar wax in the double boiler.

2 Once the wax has melted and is at about 70°C (158°F), decant the melted wax into the metal jug. Add the pale pink candle dye to the jug and stir gently until the dye has dissolved.

3 Let the wax cool slightly to around 60°C (140°F). Add the rose petal fragrance oil to the jug and stir.

4 Slowly pour the wax into the clamshell mould compartments.

5 Now leave the wax to set fully (**a**). Depending on the ambient temperature, this will take about two hours (**b**).

6 To use a wax melt, simply remove it from the clamshell mould and place onto your wax melter or oil burner.

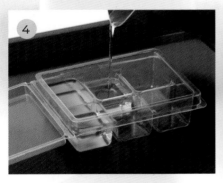

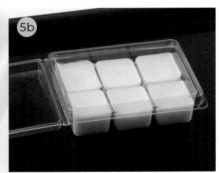

Opposite
The finished melts in use
Experiment with different fragrances to find the one that best suits you.

You will need:

- **CONTAINER** Glass votive holder (6.5cm/2½in height, 5.5cm/2¼in diameter)
- **WAX** 80g (2¾oz) soy container wax
- **WICK** Wedo ECO 4, primed, and sustainer
- Double boiler
- Glue dot
- Measuring jug
- Metal jug
- Scales
- Scissors
- Spoon
- Thermometer
- Wicking sticks

GLASS VOTIVE

Glass votive candles are very versatile and elegant. For this project we are using a glass votive holder that has been painted silver, to create a sophisticated candle that would look stunning on a wedding table.

INSTRUCTIONS

1 Melt the soy container wax in the double boiler.

2 Prepare the wick and sustainer. Fix the sustainer to the base of the glass votive holder with a glue dot.

3 Secure the top of the wick with wicking sticks.

4 Once the wax has melted and is around 70°C (158°F), decant the melted wax into the metal jug.

5 Let the wax cool slightly to around 60°C (140°F), then slowly pour the wax into the glass votive holder, leaving a 1cm (½in) gap at the top.

6 Leave the candle to set. Depending on the ambient temperature, this will take about one hour.

7 Once the candle has set, remove the wicking sticks and trim the wick to 5mm (¼in).

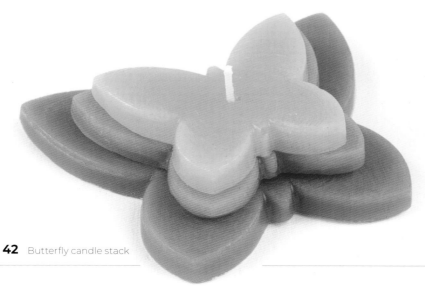

You will need:

- **MOULD** Butterfly candle mould tray
- **WAX** 75g (2¾oz) petroleum pillar wax
- **WICK** WickWell P2-46, primed, and sustainer
- **DYE** Pink candle dye (see page 18 for directions on calculating amount of dye)
- Double boiler
- Measuring jug
- Metal jug
- Oven gloves
- Scales
- Scissors
- Spoon
- Thermometer
- Wicking pin

BUTTERFLY CANDLE STACK

Candle stacks are multiple layers of thin wax which are then threaded together with a wick to make a candle. For this project I am using a butterfly mould to make up the layers.

INSTRUCTIONS

1 Melt the petroleum pillar wax in the double boiler.

2 Prepare the wick and sustainer.

3 Once the wax has melted and is at about 80°C (176°F), decant the melted wax into the metal jug.

4 Add a quarter of the pink candle dye to the jug and stir gently until the dye has dissolved. Dye chips can be snapped in half and into quarters for this purpose.

5 Slowly pour the wax into the smallest of the butterfly shapes.

6 Now add half of the remaining candle dye to the jug and stir gently until dissolved.

7 Slowly pour the wax into the medium-sized shape.

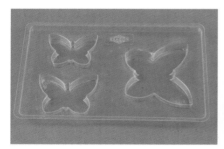

Butterfly candle mould tray

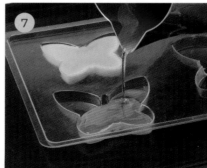

8 Add the remaining candle dye to the jug and stir gently. Then pour the rest of the wax into the largest of the butterfly shapes.

9 Leave the wax to set. Depending on the ambient temperature, this will take about one hour.

10 Release the butterfly shapes from the mould.

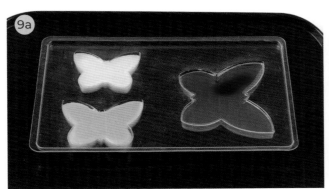

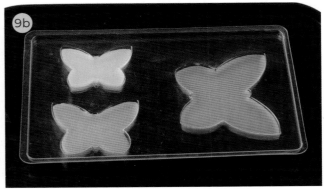

11 Heat the pointed end of a wicking pin or skewer over the flame from a lit candle. Push the wicking pin through the middle of each of the butterfly shapes to make a hole large enough to thread your wick through.

12 Thread the wick upwards through the holes of the three butterflies. Start with the largest butterfly first, so that the sustainer sits underneath the largest butterfly.

13 Next, thread the wick through the hole in the medium butterfly, then the smallest.

14 Lastly, trim the wick to 5mm (¼in).

IMPORTANT NOTE

Be very careful when heating a wicking pin or skewer over a flame as the metal will heat up quickly. To avoid burning your fingers hold the pin or skewer with an oven glove, or heat it only for a few seconds. Always supervise children with this part of the project.

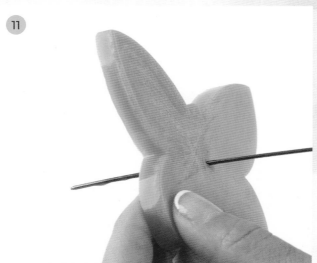

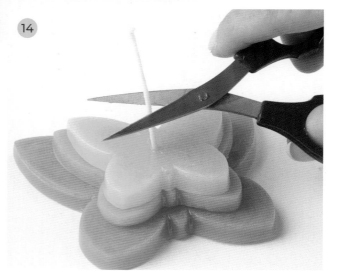

GEL CANDLE

You will need:

- **CONTAINER** Glass tumbler (9cm/3½in height, 8cm/3¼in diameter)
- **WAX** 225g (8oz) gel wax
- **WICK** Wedo RRD55, primed, and sustainer. The wick should be primed using gel wax.
- Coloured glass beads
- Double boiler
- Measuring jug
- Metal jug
- Scales
- Scissors
- Spoon
- Thermometer
- Wicking sticks

As gel candles are transparent, their flames appear to float in mid-air. For decoration we have placed some glass beads in the bottom of a glass tumbler, which can be seen through the gel. As the candle burns, the light reflects beautifully off the coloured beads, creating a pretty, aquatic effect.

INSTRUCTIONS

1 Melt the gel in the double boiler.

2 Prepare the wick and sustainer and fix the sustainer to the base of the glass tumbler with a glue dot. Secure the top of the wick with wicking sticks. As the gel is transparent make sure the wick is taut and centred as the wick will still be visible when the candle has set.

3 Pour the glass beads into the glass tumbler, filling it up to about 4cm (1½in).

4 Once the gel has melted and is at 75°C (167°F), decant the melted gel into the metal jug.

5 Slowly pour the gel into the glass tumbler.

6 Leave the candle to set fully. Depending on the ambient temperature, this will take about two hours.

7 Finally, trim the wick to 5mm (¼in).

HALLOWEEN PUMPKIN

Make the perfect Halloween candle with a spooky pumpkin face.

You will need:

- **MOULD** Fluted sphere candle mould (8cm/3¼in diameter)
- **WAX** 280g (10oz) petroleum pillar wax
- **WICK** WickWell P2-50
- **DYE** Orange candle dye (see page 18 for directions on calculating amount of dye)
- Black candle paint
- Artist's fine paint brush
- Adhesive putty
- Double boiler
- Measuring jug
- Metal jug
- Scales
- Scissors
- Spoon
- Thermometer
- Wicking sticks

Black candle paint

Fluted sphere mould

INSTRUCTIONS

1 Melt the petroleum pillar wax in the double boiler.

2 Thread the wick through the tube at the bottom of the mould.

NOTE

Secure the two halves of the fluted sphere mould using foldback clips.

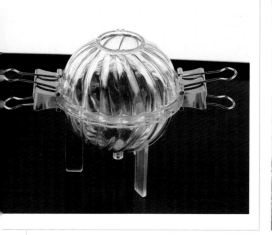

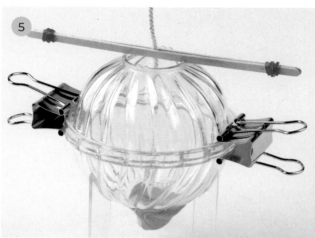

3 Tie a knot in the wick at the base of the mould.

4 Secure the knot with adhesive putty. Then turn the mould upright to rest on its 'legs'.

5 Attach the wicking sticks. Ensure the wick is centred and upright inside the mould.

6 Once the wax has melted and is at 80°C (176°F), decant the melted wax into the metal jug. Add the orange candle dye to the jug and stir gently until the dye has dissolved.

7 Slowly pour the wax into the fluted sphere mould. Save a small amount of wax in the jug to fill any dips or air pockets that appear in the candle base. Gently tap the mould to release any air bubbles.

8 Leave the candle to set fully. Depending on the ambient temperature, this will take about two hours.

9 When the candle has set, remove the foldback clips and wicking sticks, turn the mould upside-down, remove the adhesive putty and untie the knot.

10 Open the top half of the mould to release the candle, which should pop out easily.

11 Trim the top wick to 5mm (¼in). Trim the bottom wick to the base of the candle.

12 Finally, paint a pumpkin face onto the candle using an artist's paint brush and the black candle paint.

Opposite

The finished candle

Perfect for a spooktacular Halloween party, or to welcome trick-or-treaters!

FLOATING MAPLE LEAF CANDLES

You will need:

- **MOULD** Maple leaf candle mould tray
- **WAX** 150g (5¼oz) soy pillar wax
- **WICKS** 6 x Wedo TL25, primed, and sustainers
- Green wax crayon
- Double boiler
- Measuring jug
- Metal jug
- Scales
- Scissors
- Spoon
- Thermometer

Floating candles are a great way to decorate your table, especially at a dinner party. Fill a shallow bowl with water and place the candles carefully onto the surface. Light them to create a wonderful moving flame effect.

The colour of these candles comes from a green wax crayon. By gradually adding more of the crayon to the wax as you pour the wax into the moulds, you can create candles in different colour gradients.

Wax crayon

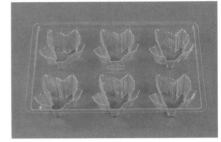
Maple leaf candle mould tray

INSTRUCTIONS

1 Melt the soy pillar wax in the double boiler.

2 Prepare the wicks and sustainers.

3 Once the wax has melted and is about 70°C (158°F), decant the melted wax into the metal jug.

4 Carefully remove any paper from the crayon. Snap a 1cm (½in) piece off the crayon and stir into the wax until the crayon has dissolved.

5 Let the wax cool slightly – to around 60°C (140°F) – then slowly pour the wax into two of the leaf moulds.

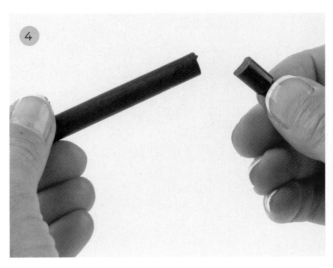

6 Lower a wick and sustainer into the centre of each of the two leaves that contain wax.

7 Add half of the remaining crayon to the wax in the metal jug and stir gently. You may need to reheat the wax using your double boiler if it has cooled below 40°C (104°F).

8 Slowly pour the wax into the mould to fill two further leaf shapes. Lower a wick and sustainer into the centre of each of these two leaves.

9 Add the remaining half of the crayon to the wax in the metal jug and stir.

10 Slowly pour the wax into the remaining two empty leaf moulds and place the wicks in the centre of each of the leaves.

11 Now leave the candles to set. Depending on the ambient temperature, this will take about one hour.

12 Once set, the candles will have shrunk slightly, so you can easily remove them from the candle moulds. Finally, trim each wick to 5mm (¼in).

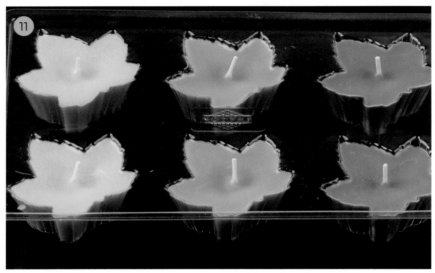

Opposite

The finished candles

Place the maple leaf candles in a bowl of water and light to create a calming ambience for a blissful summer barbecue or garden party.

CHRISTMAS PUDDING

You will need:

- **MOULD** Sphere candle mould (8cm/3¼in diameter)
- **WAX** 450g (15¾oz) soy pillar wax 2 appliqué wax sheets, red and green (see page 74)
- **WICK** Wedo ECO 2
- **DYE** Brown candle dye (see page 18 for directions on calculating amount of dye)
- Adhesive putty
- Baking tray
- Double boiler
- Heat-resistant bowl
- Measuring jug
- Metal jug
- Scissors
- Spoon
- Thermometer
- Wicking sticks
- Foldback clips
- Optional: holly sugarcraft cutter

Also known as plum pudding, or figgy pudding, the traditional British Christmas pudding, in its round incarnation, is thought by many to represent the world.

This candle is great fun to make, looks almost as good as a real Christmas pudding and is sure to set someone's world on fire if given as a gift!

INSTRUCTIONS

1 Melt 280g (10oz) of soy pillar wax in the double boiler.

2 Thread the wick through the tube at the bottom of the mould and tie a knot in the wick underneath the mould (see pages 48–49 for more advice). Secure the wick in place with adhesive putty then turn the mould upright again. Attach wicking sticks at the top of the mould. To keep the two halves of the sphere mould together securely, attach foldback clips.

3 Once the wax has melted and is at about 70°C (158°F), decant the melted wax into the metal jug.

4 Let the wax cool slightly to 60°C (140°F). Once it has reached this temperature slowly pour the wax into the sphere mould. Save a small amount of wax in the jug to fill any dips that appear in the candle base.

5 Gently tap the mould to release any air bubbles and check the wick is centred.

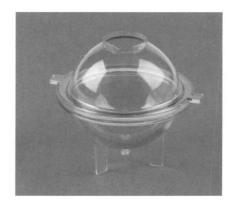

Sphere candle mould

Appliqué wax sheets

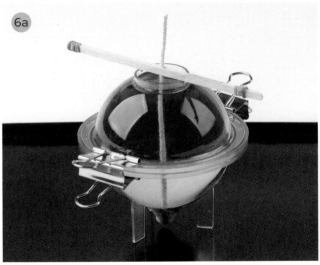

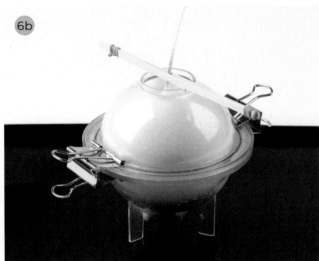

6 Leave the candle to set fully. Depending on the ambient temperature, this will take about two hours.

7 Sometimes, once the candle has set, the base of the candle (which will be uppermost in the mould) may have shrunk and become slightly concave or have holes (air pockets). If this happens, reheat the wax you saved earlier and pour this into the concave dip or holes.

8 When the candle has set, remove the foldback clips and wicking sticks, turn the mould upside-down, remove the adhesive putty and untie the knot. Do not cut the wick yet!

9 The candle will have shrunk slightly so should easily slide out of the mould. Trim the bottom wick flush with the base of the candle.

10 Melt 100g (3½oz) soy pillar wax in the double boiler.

11 Once the wax has melted and is at 70°C (158°F) decant into the heat-resistant bowl. Add the brown candle dye to the bowl and stir gently until the dye has dissolved.

TIP

Hold the wick firmly when you are dipping the candle into the brown wax. The last thing you want to do is drop the candle into the wax!

12 Holding the top of the wick of the sphere candle, dip the bottom half of the sphere into the bowl of brown wax for about five seconds. Lift out and allow the wax to drip back into the bowl. Allow to cool for one minute.

13 Repeat the dipping action until the bottom half of the sphere is dark brown.

14 Melt 100g (3½oz) soy pillar wax in the double boiler.

15 Once the wax has melted and is at about 70°C (158°F), decant into a metal jug.

16 Place the candle on a baking tray. Use a spoon to pour the wax over the top of the candle so it looks like poured custard. Leave the candle to set.

17 Take up the green appliqué wax sheet. Remove its backing sheet and, using scissors, cut out two small triangles roughly 2 x 1 x 1cm (¾ x ½ x ½in) to form holly leaves. Alternatively, if you have a holly sugarcraft cutter, cut out two holly shapes with this instead.

18 Next, tear off a little wax from the red appliqué sheet. Roll out three red, pea-sized balls for holly berries.

19 Place the leaves and berries on top of the candle.

20 Finally, trim the wick to 5mm (¼in).

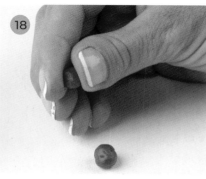

DIPPED TAPER CANDLES

Dipped tapers are the most traditional candles. The technique described here has hardly changed over the centuries and involves dipping a wick into hot melted wax, letting it cool and dipping it again.

You will need:

- **WAX** 500g (17¾oz) petroleum pillar wax (depending on the size of your dipping pot)
- **WICK** WickWell P2-46
- **DYE** Royal blue candle dye (see page 18 for directions on calculating amount of dye)
- Heat-resistant mat
- Metal trivet
- Oven gloves
- Scissors
- Tall metal dipping pot
- Tall saucepan
- Thermometer

INSTRUCTIONS

1 Set up a double boiler using a tall saucepan and dipping pot. Place the trivet in the tall saucepan. Fill the pan with two-thirds water and bring it to the boil. Sit the dipping pot in the tall saucepan on top of the metal trivet.

2 Fill the dipping pot with petroleum wax. As the wax melts, add more wax until the pot is about 90 per cent full.

3 Once the wax has melted and is at 80°C (176°F), carefully lift the dipping pot out of the saucepan with an oven glove and place on a heat-resistant mat.

4 Add the royal blue candle dye to the dipping pot and stir gently until the dye has dissolved.

NOTE

The trivet is very important: without it you would be using direct heat to melt your wax, which would be dangerous.

Metal trivet

DETERMINING THE LENGTH OF YOUR WICK

Your wick needs to be twice the height of the dipping pot, plus 5cm (2in).

For example, if your dipping pot is 25cm (9¾in) high, the total length of the wick should be:
(2 x 25cm = 50cm) + 5cm = 55cm
(2 x 9¾in = 19½in) + 2in = 21½in

TIP

When you begin to dip the wicks they will start off slightly crooked. After you've dipped them five or six times, start to pull the wicks taut after each dip and hold them in this position for about 10 seconds. Continue to do this for the next 10 to 15 dips until the candles are slightly thicker and can maintain their own shape. Practice makes perfect!

5 Fold the wick in half and hold in the middle. You now have two wicks that are joined in the middle.

6 Dip the wicks into the wax and leave for about a minute. You will see bubbles coming from the wicks: once these bubbles stop appearing, pull the wicks out of the wax. Allow the wax to drip back into the pot. Pull the wicks taut and allow to cool for three minutes.

7 Dip the wicks into the pot again for about 15 seconds and lift out. Pull the wicks taut (as before) and allow to cool.

8 Continue dipping your tapers and allowing to cool. You will want to dip them around 30 to 40 times, depending on how thick you want your candles to be.

9 When you are happy with the thickness of your candles, hang them up to let them cool. Once they are fully cooled, use scissors to cut the wick in half, and separate the two candles. Then trim each wick to 5mm (¼in).

You will need:

- **MOULD** Square metal mould, 9 x 7.5cm (3½ x 3in)
- **WAX** 430g (15¼oz) soy pillar wax
- **WICK** Wedo ECO 4
- **DYE** Turquoise candle dye (see page 18 for directions on calculating amount of dye)
- Bag of ice
- Adhesive putty
- Double boiler
- Measuring jug
- Metal jug
- Rolling pin
- Scales
- Scissors
- Spoon
- Tea towel or kitchen paper
- Thermometer
- Wicking pin

ICE PILLAR CANDLE

Ice pillar candles are fun to make. Each one is unique and they are a good talking point for visitors as they successfully combine two conflicting elements: fire and ice!

INSTRUCTIONS

1 Melt the soy pillar wax in the double boiler.

2 Prepare and secure the wick.

3 Once the wax has melted and is around 70°C (158°F), decant the melted wax into the metal jug. Add the turquoise candle dye to the jug and stir gently until the dye has dissolved.

4 Crush the ice into small pieces with a rolling pin.

5 Now spoon the ice into the candle mould to about one-third of the height of the mould.

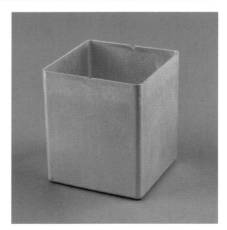

Square metal mould

NOTE

For this project we are using a wicking pin, although wicking sticks are equally suitable.

6 Check the temperature of the wax. For this project you need the wax slightly hotter so it should be around 70°C (158°F).

7 Slowly pour the wax into the mould, up to the level of the ice.

8 Spoon another third of ice into the mould, then pour the wax again. Repeat this process until you have filled the candle mould. Keep a small amount of wax in reserve.

9 Leave the candle to set fully. Depending on the ambient room temperature this will take about two hours.

10 When the candle has set, remove the wicking pin, turn the mould upside-down, remove the adhesive putty and untie the knot.

11 The candle will have shrunk slightly so should easily slide out of the mould.

12 Leave the candle on some kitchen paper or a towel and leave for two hours to allow the water to evaporate and the candle to set.

13 Finally, trim the wick to 5mm (¼in).

Opposite

The finished candle

Ice pillar candles do not always burn particularly well, as they are full of air pockets, but they do make great table decorations!

You will need:

- **CONTAINER** Glass tumbler (9cm/3½in height, 8cm/3¼in diameter)
- **WAX** 225g (8oz) petroleum container wax (75g/2¾oz per layer for three layers)
- **WICK** WickWell P2-66, primed, and sustainer
- **DYE** Light blue, grey and royal blue candle dye (see page 18 for directions on calculating amount of dye)
- Adhesive putty
- Double boiler
- Glue dot
- Measuring jug
- Metal jug
- Scales
- Scissors
- Spoon
- Thermometer
- Wicking sticks

LAYERED GLASS TUMBLER CANDLE

By tilting the candle container and adding different coloured waxes in stages, you can create a fabulous layered effect.

INSTRUCTIONS

1 Melt 75g (2¾oz) petroleum container wax in the double boiler.

2 Prepare the wick and sustainer and fix the sustainer to the base of the glass tumbler with a glue dot. Secure the top of the wick with wicking sticks.

3 Once the wax has melted and is at 80°C (176°F), decant the melted wax into the metal jug. Add the light blue candle dye to the jug and stir gently until the dye has dissolved.

4 Tilt the glass tumbler at an angle facing right and hold in position using adhesive putty.

5 Slowly pour the wax into the glass tumbler.

6 Once the candle has started to set, melt another 75g (2¾oz) of petroleum container wax in the double boiler.

7 Once the wax has melted and is around 80°C (176°F), decant the melted wax into the metal jug. Add the grey candle dye to the jug and stir gently until the dye has dissolved.

8 Tilt the tumbler in the opposite direction. Use adhesive putty to hold it in position. Slowly pour the grey wax into the tumbler.

9 Once the candle has started to set, melt another 75g (2¾oz) of petroleum container wax in the double boiler.

10 Once the wax has melted and is around 80°C (176°F), decant the melted wax into the metal jug. Add the royal blue candle dye to the jug and stir gently until the dye has dissolved.

11 Remove the adhesive putty and stand the glass tumbler flat.

12 Slowly pour the royal blue wax into the glass tumbler.

13 Now leave the candle to set. Depending on the ambient temperature, this will take about two hours.

14 Once set, remove the wicking sticks and trim the wick to 5mm (¼in).

The finished candle

Why not change the angles and add more colours to create different designs? Also, try pouring the second layer of wax before the previous layer has set fully to blend the two colours together.

WAX CHIP PILLAR CANDLE

This is one of my favourite candles to make – and I love the fact that every candle is unique. This technique creates a sort of marble effect. It takes a while to prepare, but I am sure you will find it is well worth the effort!

INSTRUCTIONS

1 Prepare the candle chips. Melt 250g (8¾oz) soy pillar wax in the double boiler.

2 Once the wax has melted and is at 70°C (158°F), decant the melted wax into the metal jug. Add the candle dye to the jug and stir gently until the dye has dissolved.

3 The temperature of the wax should now be around 60°C (140°F). If not, wait for it to cool to this temperature. Slowly pour the wax onto the baking tray.

4 Now leave the wax to set fully. Depending on the ambient temperature, this will take about two hours.

5 Take the wax out of the baking tray and break up into about 1cm (½in)-sized pieces.

6 Repeat steps 1 to 5 for the other colours. If you have more than one baking tray you can speed this up by making up the other colours at the same time.

7 Now melt 400g (14oz) soy pillar wax in the double boiler.

8 Prepare the wick and secure the wick to the mould.

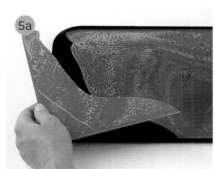

You will need:

- **MOULD** Cylindrical polycarbonate mould (8cm/3¼in diameter, 12cm/4¾in height)
- **WAX** 400g (14oz) soy pillar wax (for the mould), 1,750g (62oz) soy pillar wax (for the chips – this amount will make extra chips for future use)
- **WICK** Wedo ECO 4
- **DYE** Candle dye in seven colours: red, orange, yellow, green, blue, purple, pink (see page 18 for directions on calculating amount of dye)
- Adhesive putty
- Baking tray
- Double boiler
- Measuring jug
- Metal jug
- Spoon
- Scales
- Scissors
- Thermometer
- Wicking sticks

Cylindrical mould

9 Take the red candle chips and drop them into the candle mould; fill up to about 2cm (¾in) high.

10 Check the temperature of the wax in the double boiler. It should now be around 60°C (140°F). If it is too hot, wait for it to cool to this temperature. Slowly pour the liquid wax over the wax chips.

11 Now repeat with the orange candle chips. Carefully drop them into the mould to a height of 4cm (1½in), then pour the melted wax over the top (as in the previous step).

12 Repeat this process until you have filled the candle mould to the top. Save a small amount of wax in the jug to fill any dips that appear in the candle base.

13 Now leave the candle to set fully. Depending on the ambient temperature, this will take about two hours.

14 When the candle has set, remove the wicking sticks, turn the mould upside-down, remove the adhesive putty and untie the knot. The candle will have shrunk slightly so should easily slide out of the mould.

15 Finally, trim the wick to 5mm (¼in).

TIP

Sometimes you may find the base of the candle is slightly uneven. If this happens, carefully place the candle base in the top pan of the double boiler for a few seconds. Move the candle around in a circular motion – this will melt the base and make it smooth and flat.

Opposite
The finished candle

Why not experiment with more, or fewer, coloured chips and co-ordinate the colour of your candle to your own home?

UPCYCLING AND RECYCLING

Candle-making does not need to be expensive. You can upcycle and recycle glasses, jars, tins and tubs to make a candle. Here are a few ideas: all you need now is to follow the instructions and techniques from the previous projects, adhere to the safety instructions, use your newfound candle-making skills and apply your imagination to make some fun and inexpensive candles!

CONTAINER CANDLES

Make sure any container you recycle can withstand hot wax. One way of doing this is to place the jar in your kitchen sink and slowly pour in hot water at around 90°C (194°F). If the container does not crack it should be fine with melted wax below that temperature – but don't forget to burn test every new type of candle.

Jam jars

These are a readily available and affordable container for the beginner to candle-making. Use the method for creating a glass tumbler candle (see page 66) to make jam jar candles by sticking a sustainer and wick to the inside base using a glue dot, and filling the jar with coloured, fragranced container wax.

Glass ramekins

Use small glass dishes from desserts and pâtés to create attractive container candles for a dinner, or wedding, table.

Bottle tops

Place miniature drink cap and bottle top candles on a glass plate or mirror to make charming decorations for a dinner table. They will only burn for about an hour, however, so you will need to make plenty of them.

PILLAR CANDLES

Breadstick tube

Use these tubes to create elegant pillar candles that are not unlike expensive church candles. Although these candles do not require support or a container, they would look glamorous on a small dish, or mounted in a hurricane candle-holder.

Fresh pasta sauce container

Add candle dye and citronella fragrance to make a sturdy candle that works perfectly outdoors on a summer's evening, or at a picnic.

DECORATING YOUR CANDLES

The simplest of candles can be given an elaborate flourish with additional decoration. Here are just some of the ways in which you can enhance your creations simply and inexpensively.

APPLIQUÉ SHEETS

These very thin, self-adhesive sheets of wax can be cut into intricate shapes with sugarcraft cutters used for decorating cakes, or scissors as shown, and then pressed onto the candle.

CANDLE PAINT

You can buy candle paint that comes in the form of liquid paint or in pens. Paint or draw straight onto the candle to create your own personal design.

DRIED FLOWERS

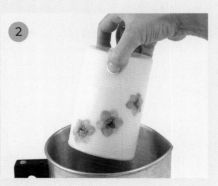

1 Heat the back of a metal teaspoon over a candle flame. Place a dried flower on the outside of a pillar candle. Press the back of the spoon onto the flower. This will melt the wax slightly so the flower will stick to the candle.

2 Once you have added more flowers and completed your design, overdip the candle to seal the flowers. Melt the overdip wax using a double boiler. Hold the candle at the top and dip the candle into the overdip wax for a second or two. Pull the candle out and allow it to cool for a few seconds.

WATER TRANSFERS

These can be purchased from specialist suppliers, and work in a similar way to temporary tattoos.

The decorated candle

1 Cut out your desired water transfer designs.

2 Soak the individual motifs in water for one minute.

3 Peel off the backing sheets from the motifs and press the designs one by one onto your candle.

RIBBON AND RAFFIA

You can decorate the outside of a glass container with ribbon, raffia or string.

Craft shops supply lots of decorations for card-making – these make attractive accessories. In the photograph on the right, a miniature decorative rose has been tied onto the candle with a length of raffia.

Remember to remove all decorative items before lighting the candle.

PACKAGING YOUR CANDLES

There are also many ways that you can decorate your finished candles to give them a professional touch. Remember that you will need to burn test thoroughly any candle that you plan to give away or sell.

CARDBOARD BOXES

You can purchase attractive boxes from craft and gift shops – simply place your finished candle inside, perhaps with some tissue or shredded paper. You can even fragrance the paper with diluted oil to match your candle.

ORGANZA BAGS

An organza bag and a label can make lovely packaging if you are giving the candle as a gift. Why not create your own logo and add the recipient's name?

BURN TESTING

If you decide to give your candles to friends or sell them you must always burn test an example first to ensure it burns well, especially if it's a new type of candle: light one of the finished candles and watch how it burns, checking the melt pool, scent throw and size of the flame.

Candles take a while to cure: it is best to let candles set fully for at least 24 hours before lighting – and ideally you should leave them for several days before beginning the test. Use these checklists to help you observe and monitor the burn-testing process:

TIP

Always label your candles and containers before you start your burn testing.

Date: __ / __ / __

Mould/container: _____

Wick type: _____

Amount of wax: _____ g/ _____ oz

Type of fragrance oil: _____

Amount of fragrance oil: _____ ml/ _____ fl.oz

Amount of dye: _____ g/ _____ oz

Room temperature: _____ °C/ _____ °F

Temperature of poured wax: _____ °C/ _____ °F

Time taken to set: _____ hrs: _____ mins:

Candle characteristics (e.g. size of flame, strength of scent throw, presence of air bubbles):

_____

_____

_____

_____

_____

_____

Start of burn (time): __ : __

End of burn (time): __ : __

You should burn the candle for three hours. After three hours you should extinguish the candle and let it cool and set before you relight it.

TIME	SCENT THROW (COLD)	SCENT THROW (HOT)	FLAME HEIGHT (cm/in)	AMOUNT OF SOOT (g/oz)	MELT POOL SIZE, DEPTH & DIAMETER (cm/in)
30 mins					
1 hour					
2 hours					
3 hours					
Allow to cool and set					
30 mins					
1 hour					
2 hours					
3 hours					
Allow to cool and set					
30 mins					
1 hour					
2 hours					
3 hours					

TROUBLESHOOTING

PROBLEM	POSSIBLE SOLUTION
Candle burns too fast	The wick is too thick. Try using a smaller, thinner wick.
Candle drips	Ensure the candle is not close to a draught. Use a smaller wick, or a different type of wick.
Flame flickers or splutters	Check there is no water in the mould. Check for air bubbles in the wax. Ensure the wick is primed (see Techniques, page 16). Reduce the amount of fragrance oil you use.
Candle will not light	Ensure the wick is primed.
Small flame	The wick is trimmed too short. The wick is too small. You are using the wrong type of wick (some wicks are uni-directional – they have a top and a bottom – and work better one way).
Small melt pool	The wick is too small – use a larger or thicker wick.
Flame extinguishes	Air bubbles are released from the wax and blow out the flame. The wick is too small – try a slightly larger or thicker wick.
Soot or mushrooming	These issues can be caused by impurities in the wax or too much fragrance oil depositing on the wick. Use less fragrance oil or change the blend if you have mixed two oils. Check with the manufacturer that fragrance oil is compatible with the wax. Soot or mushrooming (see page 11) can also be caused by poor-quality or recycled wax. Use pure, or high-quality waxes as detailed in Tools and materials, pages 8–9. Use a smaller or thinner wick.
Air bubbles and craters	These happen when you pour or stir wax too quickly. Always stir and pour wax slowly. Tap the mould after pouring wax to release air bubbles. Try pouring wax at a slightly cooler temperature.
Coloured wax runs together	Allow the first wax pour to set slightly before pouring the second coloured wax. When making pillar candles, make sure the first layer has not set solid – it may have shrunk slightly, which would allow the second pour of wax to flow into the gap between the candle and the mould.
Candle 'sweats' beads of oil/wax	Use less fragrance oil. Use a different fragrance oil – it may be incompatible with the wax.
Side of candle looks damp	The candle has cooled too quickly. Allow the candle to cool at room temperature. Warm the candle container slightly before pouring in the wax.
Candle stuck in mould	The wrong kind of wax may have been used (i.e. container wax has been used in a pillar mould). Immerse the container and candle carefully in hot water (around 70°C/158°F). Be careful not to scald yourself.

INDEX